YOU'RE WHAT YOU THINK

"7 Principles to Creating the Life
You've Always Wanted"

By
Pamela Ennis

You Are What You Think
"7 Principles to Creating The Life You've Always Wanted"
By Pamela Ennis

Readapy books may be ordered through booksellers or by contacting:

Readapy Publishing Company
Hollywood, CA
www.readapy.com
1-240-350-9234

Because of the nature of the Internet, any web addresses or links contained in this book may have changed since publication and may no longer be valid.

The views expressed in this work are solely those of the author and do not necessarily reflect the views of the publisher, hereby disclaims any responsibility for them.

This book is dedicated to my husband Mike and my three beautiful children: Serigne, Solomon and Sarah, who inspire me to no end. Darlings, your unconditional love has given me wings of an eagle and allowed me to soar the highest of heights.

To be yourself in a world that is constantly trying to make you something else is the greatest accomplishment.

— Ralph Waldo Emerson

TABLE OF CONTENTS

ACKNOWLEDGMENTS

I give thanks to God and all of my family and friends who have had faith in me, provided encouragement and support, and challenged me along my journey. A special thanks to my mother, Marian Smith, one of the wisest people I know; thank you for all of your love and support.

I would not be true to myself or the pages of this book without giving thanks to many of the authors and spiritual leaders who have inspired me and played a significant role in my spiritual shift in consciousness by revealing truths that forced me to release conformity, embrace awareness and open up to my fullest potential.

Reverend Lonnie R. Freeman where it all began, Dr. Richard Taylor who laid the foundation, Dr. Michael Bernard Beckwith, and Deepak Chopra—you are modern-day sages who are paving the way to higher truths. Continued blessing to you all.

INTRODUCTION

You have within your possession right now, today, a power that goes beyond your human intellect—a power that, once unlocked, can change your life forever. The intent of *You Are What You Think: "7 Principles to Creating The Life You've Always Wanted"* is to show you how to discover the power within. You can begin to experience immediate changes, and ultimately create the life you've always wanted. The results that you will see as you begin to apply the principles in this book will astonish you to no end. When I realized I'd stumbled onto the *"Guaranteed"* 7 Principles to success, it took me a minute to fully understand what was really happening and what I was doing to obtain all of the things I was creating in my life. In a way, I took it for granted and never really gave any thought to the fact that I was able to achieve and acquire just about anything. It was the people around me, family, friends and colleagues, who over the years constantly brought it to my attention. They would say things like "Wow, you're so lucky" or "You've really found favor with God," or "How do you do it?" I could go on and on to tell you of my experiences of how I've received the things that I've wanted for many years; however, that's not the goal of this book. As stated earlier, the goal is to show you how to do the same thing.

What you will learn by reading this book will be unlike any experience you've ever encountered. If you've purchased this book, if it was given to you or if you're holding it in your hand and can't remember from whence it came, I ask only three things of you:

1. *Believe with all of your heart that it was meant for you to have this book, right now, this day, and at this time in your life.*
2. *Believe that it is your time to discover 7 Principles of the ages and unveil the power to create the life you've always wanted.*
3. *Be prepared to transform your life.*

Pamela Ennis, PhD

How To Use This Book

This book is divided into seven core spiritual principles that are necessary for you to begin experiencing the life you want. Each principle is designed to give you a foundation and a simple but thorough understanding of its meaning. At the end of each chapter you will be provided with "Action Guidelines" that are *required* to put into practice immediately upon completion of that chapter.

The "Action Guidelines" at the end of each chapter are an integral part of the process and should not be skipped. It is also recommended that you make sure you fully understand the principle and its foundation before moving on to the next chapter, because the principles in this book are built upon progression from chapter to chapter.

Do not try to implement every concept at once. If you find that you are rushed, unfocused or preoccupied, I suggest that you put the book away until you have quiet time to spend reading. What you will learn here are spiritual principles that have been in existence for thousands of years; each principle will be at the heart of your experience. The *value* of the principles contained within these pages cannot truly be contained in one book, so it's very important that you spend time fully understanding each principle before moving on to the next.

Wisdom is the principal thing; therefore get wisdom: and with all your getting get understanding.

—**Proverbs 4:7**

CHAPTER 1
MAKE UP YOUR MIND

Before we begin I would like to ask you to set aside all of your previously held theories and beliefs. Take a minute and think about how wonderful life would be if you had an instant remedy for releasing those things that continuously keep you from achieving what we really want in life. How would you feel if I told you that the first 7 Principles to transforming your life and having all that you want is to *make up your mind* about what it is that you want? Yes, principle number one is just that simple.

Your mind was designed to create. Many thoughts that you have will in some way manifest into reality. Everything we see in form was once just a thought. The computer that I'm using to type this manuscript once existed only as a thought. The chair that I'm sitting in was once only a thought. In reality all things that appear to us visually were once thoughts that have manifested themselves into reality.

Deepak Chopra in the *"The Seven Laws of Spiritual Success"* says: "All of creation, everything that exists in the physical world, is the result of the un-manifest becoming manifest." If this is true, and I believe it is, what that means is that all of the negative habits and patterns that are currently in our lives once existed only as a thought, and if we can find a way to eliminate or change that thought, we can eliminate or change that negative pattern. This is not the type of teaching that our society has provided us with over the years; in fact, society has taught us the total opposite of this principle.

As children, we are not only taught to mimic our parents, but we're also constantly told that we are just like our parents. How many times have you been told, "you're acting just like your father or you're acting just like your mother?" It's okay to be just like your father or mother if Mom and Dad have healthy habits and healthy thought lives. On the other hand, if as a result of their thought life Mom and Dad have created unhealthy patterns and habits; then it's not okay to be just like them; to be more exact, it's not okay to *think* just like them. Keep in mind that the statement "You're just like your father/mother" existed first in thought only; as it was spoken, it was manifested into reality, and now you're actually experiencing and are exhibiting those patterns and behaviors.

In my own life I've often noticed patterns of behavior that remind me so much of my mother, some good, some not so good. However, it's a true reality check when your kid says to you, "Mom, you're acting just like Granny." Every time I heard one of those statements it was generally when I was not projecting in a positive light; I would take a step back to identify the thought or time in my life where that pattern of behavior could've began and I immediately start practicing the process of eliminating and replacing those behavior patterns with more positive ones.

There is a universal law of *cause and effect* that basically states, "For every action there is a reaction." In Christianity, it's referred to as "reaping and sowing." In Eastern religions it's referred to as "karma" and most recently it's being referred to as "Law of Attraction". Although it's been said many times, in many ways, it still comes back to "whatever you put out there, whether in thought or in deed, will come back to you." If I fail to get any other point across in this book, I do hope that my audience will receive this one. If we all could grasp this one simple universal law, we would have already won half the battle.

The principles behind you are what you think, and creating the life you've always wanted through the process of managing your thought life has become and will continue to be the main focus of my message. It's my story, my song, and I will tell it everywhere I go. I see so many people needlessly suffering from physical, mental and spiritual stress, all due to not fully understanding the universal principles and spiritual laws that govern the way we think.

Now that you understand the importance of managing what and how you are thinking and that your thoughts can ultimately cause you to experience a particular environment or circumstance, we can move on to the why and how of making up your mind about what it is that you really want out of life.

In case you're thinking I'm going to teach you "how to" experience and receive the life you want, I'm not. In fact, I can't. No one can teach you that, because you already know how. At every hour, every minute and every second you are *already* using your thoughts to cause both wanted and un-wanted experiences. What I am going to teach you are the principles behind this process; in doing so you will learn "how to" experience more of what you do want and not what you don't want.

First, you must choose. You must decide. You must get a good picture in your mind of what it is that you want. You must be aligned mentally, emotionally, physically and spiritually with your goal or desire in order for it to manifest. Otherwise, you are sending mixed signals. Be specific. The more specific your thoughts, the quicker they can come to past. Know whether you want a new car or a used truck. Make a commitment to your desire. Don't be wishy-washy. For example, you may say, "I wouldn't mind buying a new car, or perhaps I'll just get this one repaired or maybe I'll look at a used one." This is not *making up your mind* about what you want. This type of thought is considered wishy-washy and will only slow or totally halt the creation process. The correct statement should be: "I would like a brand-new, Silver Blue Mercedes Benz with a sunroof, leather interior and a GPS." You must also picture yourself with the Mercedes in your possession. Picture yourself driving it; imagine how you will feel with the sunroof open and the wind in your hair, or warm sun beaming down on you. The reason it's important to attach your emotions to the thought is that the more energy or feeling that you put behind your thoughts, the sooner they will manifest. Once you can see yourself driving to work in your new Mercedes, listening to your favorite radio station or audio book, you should either go to the dealer and actually look at the vehicle you want or purchase a car magazine and look for that very same car. In doing this, you are now aligning your physical actions with your mental and emotional actions.

Regardless of your religious beliefs or spiritual background, it's important for you to spend time in communion with God, there are many ways this can be accomplished. A guaranteed way to accomplish this is through prayer and meditation. Prayer and meditation will also assist you in "focusing" and by learning to focus and concentrate on what it is that you really want you will be able to co-create it a lot more quickly. Remember, your thoughts must be aligned mentally, emotionally, physically and spiritually.

I couldn't possibly go to the next chapter without first explaining how all of this works, and secondly giving you some tools to help you immediately begin the manifesting process in your life. Remember I said it's *guaranteed,* so by the time you finish this book and follow these simple guidelines there's no reason you shouldn't be on target for receiving those things you've always wanted. In fact, in the last chapter I will show how you can use the power that is already within you to bring about these manifestations. You will be able to use these principles the very same day that you finish this book.

How does this all work? Throughout the ages, people have witnessed healers and others exercising the power of the spiritual mind over matter, or "miracles," but as the twentieth century came to an end, many scientists, including five astrophysicists from different universities, agreed that they were on the brink of proving that consciousness affects matter, supporting mathematical findings in the subtle energy field research of quantum physics. Whew! Deep, right? Let me break it down even further, basically you have the power to manipulate the energy around you in any way that you choose. That's the scientific definition of how it works. Now let me give you the spiritual definition for how it works, which I'm sure will be much more palpable.

There are two selves that exist in every one of us. One is the temporary ever-changing self, the one you see when you look into the mirror, the one that has been conditioned by our parents, society and general life experiences. This self has a very limited perception of universal and spiritual truths; therefore it not only limits its appreciation for itself but it also limits its possibility. Scientists have told us for ages that man utilizes only ten percent of his brain. The reason for this is because this self doesn't even realize that the possibilities are there and that all things are possible. The other self is the *true self.* Christians call it the spirit or soul of a man and Buddhism calls it the Buddha Mind. This true self or spirit self is omnipotent, omnipresent, with no beginning and no ending. It exists everywhere, all the time, simultaneously. When you apply these principles and focus your thoughts your true self or spirit being connected to a higher power that is everywhere, all the time, simultaneously, it is able to make evident those things that were once only hoped for and your thoughts thereby become your reality. By keeping a direct, consistent contact with your true self you will begin to realize that you are not alone in your creating and that there is a higher intelligence working on your behalf. As I mentioned earlier, through meditation and prayer it will become a constant reality that you are co-creating with a higher power.

With a combination of your true self or spirit and mind working together, your thoughts and your dreams can determine what you are, what you have and what you will become. In truth, all that we are and all that we will become is a direct result of our thoughts. I have learned that I cannot blame others for my life, or my state of affairs; they are my creation, the end product of my thoughts and actions.

"Make Up Your Mind" Action Guidelines

1. *Choose: Decide what it is that you want.*

2. *Align your choice mentality emotionally, physically and spiritually.*

3. *Be specific: Ladies, please don't just say, "I want a husband." Oh, you will get one alright, but he may not be the one you want, so be specific!*

4. *Use Your Imagination: Picture yourself experiencing your choice.*

5. *Put your thoughts into action.*

6. *Physical realities come forth as a result of your thinking and alignment with spiritual and universal truth. As you have a creative idea or thought or inspiration, immediately say to yourself, "My true self puts this thought into action immediately."*

7. *Stay connected to your true self: Remember, this will be your co-partnership with the Spirit of God who knows everything and is everywhere all of the time, simultaneously.*

CHAPTER 2

RIGHT THOUGHTS

Principle 1 showed you how to use your thought process along with spiritual alignment to create a *specific* experience in your life. Now we will move on to learning how to constantly have positive experiences in all that you do. This principle will show you how all of your life's goals in general can be harmoniously accomplished with *least effort*. When I say least effort I do not mean that you will not have to put forth any effort at all. What I'm saying is that you will not have to struggle and experience the worry, doubt and fear that most people encounter when going through their day-to-day lives when trying to get from point A to point B. Getting from point A to point B can be in the form of a job promotion, buying a new home, starting a new relationship or ending an old relationship that has proven to be unhealthy for your well-being. Successful living can be yours and is yours to the degree that you are aware of reality and your relationship to it.

This type of harmonious, effortless success can be obtained by establishing and maintaining the *right thoughts.* What do I mean by right thoughts? Your attitude. You will need to establish and maintain a positive mental attitude and outlook in all that you do. I rarely use the word attitude, because I think it's overused and highly misunderstood, but basically a person's attitude reflects his or her *thoughts* about who and what they are. "As a man thinketh in his heart, so is he," says Jesus Christ. What you truly believe about your life and yourself is reflected in what you show people each day. It's reflected in your speech and in your actions. People with a negative attitude are easily spotted; they are generally extremely pessimistic and highly opinionated. People with a positive attitude or *right thoughts,* as I've coined it, are encouraging, uplifting, nonjudgmental, and have an overall belief in the inherent goodness of life.

Some people, regardless of their religion, race or social background, naturally speak and think in ways that are positive and effective, while others have a habit of thinking in ineffective ways. One can often detect how deliberate a creator someone is by the way he or she expresses him or herself.

For example:
"It's a beautiful day. I hope it stays nice like this for the remainder of the week. (This is a positive person with right thoughts speaking. This type of thought will lead to more beautiful weather for this person)

"I hope it doesn't rain! It always rains every time I make plans!" This is a pessimistic person and I guarantee you it will rain. If not literally, figuratively in their surroundings. (These people generally make everyone else miserable if allowed)

"I want to create harmony and happiness in this relationship. I know we can do it and we both want it." (A very positive person with the right thoughts; continuation of these thoughts will lead to a strong healthy relationship)

"I don't want to fight with you. I hate it when we fight. I can't take this any more. This has to change!" (This response will only lead to more fighting and frustration)

A few years ago I temporarily relocated to Southern California to complete my Ph.D., here's a real-life example of the type of feedback that I received from a pessimistic person:

Me:
"I've decided to move to Los Angeles. Based on my desire to complete my studies and the opportunity to accomplish my goals, I've found that Southern California will provide me with an infinite number of options to make this happen." (This is positive thinking and speaking)

Pessimistic person's response:

"Wow, I wish I could've moved to the West Coast as well, but I hear it's so expensive out there. The job market is tight, and a tiny apartment costs what a nice house costs here in Texas. And what about those earthquakes?"

Clearly you can see where this is going. I don't need to say more about this dialogue; it's totally negative, unless one is trying to talk oneself out of it! This train of thought leads to negative, pessimistic feelings, and if the move is undertaken, undesirable experiences with finances and perhaps even earthquakes would occur. By the way, as planned, I moved to Los Angeles for two years, completed my graduate program, lived in a very nice apartment on the Marina, maintained my home in Houston and was earthquake-free. Just think if I'd allowed myself to be influenced (in a bad way) by the pessimistic person. The reason I specify "in a bad way" is that I *was* influenced by that person, but it was in a good way. It was that person, among others, who influenced me to write this book, so in that respect, I cherish that experience.

In this last example, the positive-thinking person has used right thoughts to open him/herself not only to creative problem solving, but to the limitless resources of the Spirit of God to ensure that thoughts and speaking are "in line" with their desires. The pessimistic thinker, however, sends energy in direct opposition to what is expressed as desired. Note also the difference in feeling between saying, "I wish..." which is weak and implies it's unlikely to happen, and "I've decided." Saying "I've decided" sets things strongly into motion.

There's a choice you must make in order to maintain right thoughts and a positive attitude. You can decide to base your thoughts and actions on the experiences of your ego or you can base them upon the reality of your *true self*. This true self, as we discussed in Principle 1, is the power, wisdom and spiritual intelligence that is within all of us. Once you base your thoughts and attitude on your true self or spirit man, you then have an absolute frame of reference in which to pattern your behavior. Jesus, The Christ, said, "When you see me, you see my Father." That's a powerful statement. What Christ was saying is, "I and my Father are One because I am the exact replica of his persona. I identify with His intelligence, I identify with His spirit; my actions, my thoughts are his actions and his thoughts; we are one in the same."

On the other hand, you can choose to take the road most traveled—it's a busy highway so you won't be lonely—and base your attitude on the ego. The ego trip is filled with the turmoil, confusion, pride and frustrations of the up-and-down cycles of the human experience, which, over a period of time, zap the strength and health of a person; thereby causing dependency on drugs, alcohol and other vices. An attitude based strictly on ego is destined for self-destruction in one form or another. We were not placed on this earth to allow our ego to dominate our lives. We are to be co-creators with the God's Omnipotent, Omnipresent Power if we want to live a truly fulfilling life. The negative traits and thoughts that accompany the ego are what keep a person from having the life he or she desires. Once these traits and thoughts are removed and replaced with right thoughts, success and happiness will be automatic. As mentioned in Principle 1, the influence of society and others in our earlier years helped to create the ego, and these negative thoughts have been holding you back. However, the reason you are reading this book right now, this day, is because your spirit in partnership with a higher power whom most of us know as God has designed it as such; it's time for you to take control, rid yourself of the ego and remove from your mind, once and for all, the negative thought forces that have been preventing you from obtaining the best that life has to offer.

Be assured that you have a purpose in life that you may not yet have realized. Having right thoughts and demonstrating positive traits in your attitude and personality are the key to unlocking your destiny and desired lifestyle. Just think, if nothing negative existed in your thoughts, only the strong points of your character would stand out and you'd be adored by all. Well, I wouldn't take it that far; remember there will always be some negative, pessimistic person that would have a problem with you, but you get my point. If only the strong points of your character were standing out and only the right thoughts were being released, your desires would automatically become even stronger and your ability to instantly manifest and achieve your reality would soar.

We've discussed principles for developing right thoughts, positive thinking and removing negative thoughts in order to effortlessly create positive experiences in our lives. But what if you're currently experiencing unpleasant circumstances as a result of the negative thoughts of the ego, that were set in motion prior to the learning of these principles? I'm sure you're thinking it's easy to think right thoughts about one's life when you're in a positive trend. However, we should also continue to think right thoughts even when a perceived negative situation is taking place. Do not yield to the negativity; do not fall victim to the circumstance. My mother used to have a saying: "I may fall down in a ditch, but I'm not going to lay there and wallow in it." My mother was actually using this simple "old-fashioned" phrase to practice right thoughts and positive thinking. In modern-day the translation of her words is "To yield to negativity will only create further negativity," and delay the change for the greater good that is taking place.

If you're going through a difficult situation in your life right now, perhaps financial difficulties, an unhealthy relationship or a physical challenge, now is the time to put your newfound spiritual thought power to work. As my mother used to say, "Don't lay there and wallow," and further delay your change. Use these principles by first; not allowing your thinking to become negative about yourself and your life, regardless of the situation—no matter what! You must keep your thoughts positive and realize that you are going through a transitional period that appears on the surface to be negative and destructive. Know without a doubt that the only thing being destroyed is the "old" way of thinking to clear the way for right thoughts and even greater good in your life. Think in this way during this period and your thoughts will remain positive, thereby causing the transitional period to quickly pass so that you can begin creating a whole new world filled with success and happiness. You can use this negative situation or contrast as a tool to provide you with clarity for what it is that you really want. What better way to identify what you want than to know beyond a shadow of a doubt what it is that you don't want.

If you're already in a perceived negative situation due to thoughts of the ego that have been set in motion, you should take more time to connect with your true self and God's Spirit to assist you with realizing your reality. Your reality is that you are a perfect creation made in the likeness of all that is good and all that is perfect. Realizing this reality is guaranteed to feed your surface thinking with the right thoughts; it will also program your subconscious mind daily with thoughts that will cause your situation to pass more quickly. As discussed in Principle 1, this connection can be accomplished with meditation and prayer. Taking time each day to enter into meditation and prayer will help you maintain peace, inner renewal and regeneration through contact with your innermost spiritual nature.

Once you've found peace in the midst of your situation you can then ask yourself some questions so you can find out what has caused this situation. Remember I told you in Principle 1 that you are the creator of *everything* that occurs in your life, the good and so-called bad circumstances. By asking yourself these questions you will stimulate insight and intuition from your *true self,* and bring about the realization of the causes of negative situations that are in your life. Ask yourself the following questions:

- What in my thinking has brought the present unpleasant situation?
- What in my thinking can be changed to bring about a positive new situation?
- What at this time needs to be eliminated from my life and what needs to be added to it?

- What in my life no longer serves me as it once did? A job, a relationship, a lifestyle?
- What is my *true self* trying to tell me by bringing this book to me that I'm reading right now, this day, about making positive changes in my life?

Before I provide you with the *"Right Thoughts Action Guidelines"*, I want to give you a short list that comprises some of the most common negative thoughts that can hold you back. Practice self-awareness and each time you hear, speak or think one of these negative thoughts, immediately replace it with the corresponding right thought and affirmation as listed below.

NEGATIVE THOUGHTS	RIGHT THOUGHTS
LACK OF CONFIDENCE	CONFIDENCE

"I'm confident in all that I do. I am in my *true self* a co-creator with the God who is omnipresent, therefore I can do all things."

NEGATIVE THOUGHTS	RIGHT THOUGHTS
POOR SELF IMAGE	WINNING SELF-IMAGE

"As Jesus The Christ stated, 'When you see me, you see my Father' because in REALITY, I am created in the likeness of all that is perfect and all that is good."

NEGATIVE THOUGHTS	RIGHT THOUGHTS
LACK OF EDUCATION	HIGHER WISDOM

"My knowledge does not come from this world; by walking in my *true self* I am guided by the higher Omnipresent of the living God. The world didn't give it to me and the world can't take it away."

NEGATIVE THOUGHTS	RIGHT THOUGHTS
DIFFULTY COMMUNICATING	GOOD COMMUNICATOR

"I am one with the spirit of God who is all knowing, and through communion with that presence, I am always led to say the right thing at the right time."

NEGATIVE THOUGHTS	RIGHT THOUGHTS
ANXIOUS, TENSE	RELAXED, POISED

"My relationship with God gives me peace that surpasses all understanding. I carry my peace with me wherever I go, so I am relaxed and poised at all times."

NEGATIVE THOUGHTS	RIGHT THOUGHTS
HOSTILITY	PLEASANT TO OTHERS

"Because I understand that we are all ONE created in the likeness and image of all that is perfect and all that is good, I understand that by being good to others, I am being good to an extension of myself.

NEGATIVE THOUGHTS	RIGHT THOUGHTS
POOR TIME MANAGEMENT	GOOD USE OF TIME

"I respect the time of the omnipotent power and I know that my time is his time, because at a deeper level via my *true self,* spirit man, we are one. I will make efficient use of my time for my success and happiness."

NEGATIVE THOUGHTS	RIGHT THOUGHTS
SLOVENLINESS	NEATNESS, GROOMING

"I am a beautiful representation of the Holy Spirit and I am a representation of all that is good and all that is perfect."

NEGATIVE THOUGHTS	RIGHT THOUGHTS
CONTINUAL CONFUSION	INTUITIVE DIRECTION

"I in my *true self* have a perfect mind. I have perfect understanding and thoughts that are guided by omnipotent power.

NEGATIVE THOUGHTS	RIGHT THOUGHTS
GUILT FEELINGS	FREEDOM FROM GUILT

"As I would forgive a child who has erred, I also forgive myself. I know that I am *(true self)* created in the perfect image of all that is good and it is only my ego that has caused this error."

NEGATIVE THOUGHTS	RIGHT THOUGHTS
LONELINESS	COMPASSION

"I am sensitive and responsive to the needs of others because I understand that they are an extension of myself."

NEGATIVE THOUGHTS	RIGHT THOUGHTS
"TOO OLD"	YOUTHFULNESS

"The Omnipotent Power; it has no beginning and no end. It's constantly giving birth to new ideas, keeping my thoughts youthful, and so, too, my life."

NEGATIVE THOUGHTS	RIGHT THOUGHTS
NEGATIVE PAST	POSTIVE FUTURE

"I release the past negativities of yesteryears and let them go."

NEGATIVE THOUGHTS	RIGHT THOUGHTS
HUMORLESS	SENSE OF HUMOR

"I am a beautiful, youthful creation that walks in the presence of my perfect peace. I am guided and directed by Omnipotent, Omnipresent Power. I do not carry guilt; my life is devoid of confusion, therefore I utilize every moment for my greater good. I am open and honest in my communication; however, I am yet tactful, compassionate and careful not to offend others. Because I am confident in all these things, I can enjoy the lighter and more humorous things that happen each day."

"Right Thoughts" Action Guideline

1. *Establish and maintain an overall positive attitude (right thoughts).*

2. *Choose your true self and not your ego as your frame of reference for establishing your thoughts.*

3. *"Do not wallow in a ditch." Maintain positive, right thoughts even in a perceived negative situation.*

4. *Ask yourself; what in your thoughts has caused the present situation.*

5. *Drum roll!! Please, please don't go around telling everyone what a difficult time you're having. This only builds up further negativity in your mind and will be reflected back to you physically by the people whom you are telling.*

6. *Be particularly aware of new ideas about your life that may enter your mind during this challenging time. These new ideas or information may be direct guidance from your true self in relationship with Omnipotent and Omnipresent Power. Example: This book that you're reading. Don't take it lightly. There are no coincidences. Everything that happens, happens for a reason. So it is meant for you to be reading this book, right now, this very day.*

7. *Practice self-awareness and realize that you damage yourself psychologically, psychically and spiritually if your thoughts are not positive, no matter what perceived negative situations might arise.*

CHAPTER 3
RELEASE AND LET GO!

Principle 3 will show you how to release and let go of old patterns and habits that continually stifle your growth and keep you in a place of complacency. In order to create the life you want, your thoughts must be clearly focused and direct. Most people never accomplish what they want because they do not know what they want; the reason they do not know is that they have so much junk and clutter in their minds that they can't see the forest for the trees. In fact, they can't even see trees from the old leaves that need raking up and clearing out.

The age old biblical lesson that teaches that "no man should put new clothing on an old garment or new wine into old skins," is saying that we are in constant mental, physical and spiritual development. We are continuously growing and living a new life. When the new and the old no longer coexist in harmony it is time to release and let go of the old. It does not mean that you forget about all the good that may have come from the old; in fact, it's the total opposite. We must embrace the good that came from the old truths and continue to expand upon them for our greater good.

Now, on the other hand, if the old skins and old garments brought you nothing but grief, misery, financial distress, mental and spiritual stagnation, you should release and let go as quick as you can. Of course, that's once you fully understand the principles behind how old patterns and habits take root in our lives. A pattern is not just the outer action of what you see. It is the manifestation of a psychic force in one's life. Stay with me on this one; I'm not talking psychic as in the psychic network. I mean it's an unseen force or energy that is working in a person's life that is causing the pattern. You can also replace the term "psychic force" with "spiritual force" and it could mean the same, so please let's not get lost in semantics and lose out on the message. I don't know who that last sentence was for, but one of my readers needed to hear it. Okay, moving on. Psychologists speak about the effects of positive and negative patterns in the subconscious mind; however, the principles in this book are based on the spiritual wisdom, so we have further insight into how to release and let go of these negative patterns and create new and healthier ones.

Thoughts, as we've learned in Principle 1, are energy. Therefore, when a pattern in your life is physically established it has ultimately been set up by a pattern of unseen energy forces that you've created with your thoughts. Remember in the example of the Mercedes Benz, we also talked about the power of adding physical actions in order to expedite the manifestation of your thoughts. Well, it works that same way for a pattern, whether good or bad. Once those unseen energy forces are in place mentally, they can be influenced and materialized by your physical participation in activities or the company of activities that will further perpetuate that energy pattern. In this sense our mind can motivate the body and the body can also motivate the mind to produce the desired result.

Ever noticed how; when you're in a rut, all it takes is a change of scenery or a mini-vacation and you feel all better? Nothing else has changed. You're still the same person, with the same financial woes, problems on the job, kids acting up in school, but that mini-vacation (physical action/environment) has influenced your mind and temporarily made it all seem better. However, what you will learn in Principle 3 is that you do not need to take a vacation in the physical sense to release and let go of old patterns; rather, you take a vacation and break away from certain set ways of going about the things in your daily activities that has created this perceived rut.

Not all patterns that one must eliminate have to be negative. Some may have been positive at one time, but have served their purpose and have now become more of a routine or attachment to past emotions and feelings. I call those *"patterns of nostalgia."* They generally come in the form of old relationships that is not growing or going anywhere, jobs that have just become a day-to-day routine but you're no longer getting any gratification from them, and eating dessert after every meal just because you used to do it when you were a kid. (Trust me, for an adult, to eat dessert after every meal no longer serves you.) Be careful of these types of patterns that can cling to you forever in the name of justification. By justification, I mean giving you all the reasons from the past as to why they need to remain in your life. As a rule of thumb, if none of the proposed justifications are serving you in the present, then release them and let them go. My philosophy is "if it's not growing and not going" then let it go.

When mental patterns have been active for a long period of time, there is an unseen wall that surrounds a person. This wall, although unseen, is very real and makes it very difficult for positive thoughts and experiences to penetrate. As the older generation used to say, it becomes a stronghold. In order to break this wall you will have to continue to think right thoughts, but you have to make changes to your physical activities as well. As I mentioned earlier, Principle 3 teaches us to use the body to influence the mind. If we can change the effect on our physical senses, we can affect the mind and thereby change the patterns. In the New Testament, the Apostle Paul teaches, *"Be ye transformed by the renewing of your mind."*

You will begin by changing the way that you go about your daily life. These changes will began to stimulate your nervous system and create an effect on those stagnant thoughts that have created the energy forces around the patterns. The intent here is to break down that unseen wall that is keeping any positive experiences from penetrating. If you are a person who normally shops on Saturday mornings between 10:00 a.m. and 12:00 p.m., begin to practice a change of patterns and next Saturday shop in the afternoon from 2:00 p.m. to 4:00 p.m. instead. Change or add something exciting to your diet. Perhaps you eat only seafood or you're a steak and potatoes person. Add some spice; next time you go out for dinner, try a new Middle Eastern restaurant, or perhaps just have pizza for dinner instead of a three-course meal. (I'm sure you'll be a hit with the kids for that one.)

I remember the first time I practiced Principle 3; it was very interesting, to say the least. I routinely would wake up around 7:00 a.m., meditate, get dressed and get into the office between 9:00 or 9:30 a.m. I decided I would change the time that I woke up and get into the office earlier, so for one week, I woke up at 6:00 a.m., meditated for 30 minutes instead of 15, and I was in the office by 7:30 a.m.. If only you could've seen the faces of the people in my office when I walked in at 7:30 a.m.. They couldn't believe it. What I couldn't believe was that they had me so pegged, so they thought or as I was told, "I thought you just were not a morning person".

Because each person has his or her own routine, you will need to figure out how to do things differently as you go through your day. Here are a few suggestions of activity patterns you can change:

- Shop at a different time or place than usual.
- Drive different streets than usual, to work and other places. (Make sure you have MapQuest or a GPS in that new Mercedes Benz!)
- Add some new exercises to your routine, assuming you exercise. If you don't exercise, start.
- Housecleaning. This is a big one. Throw away or give away things you no longer need, things that no longer serve you. Do not collect junk.
- Change your time of day for meditation and prayer and/or began to meditate and pray.
- Wake up at a different time and go to bed at a different time.
- If you're shopping for clothes, buy an extreme style that you would not ordinarily buy.
- If you had any negative communication with someone recently, try talking to that person in a friendly way. If that person receives you, great! If they choose to remain in the state you left them in, make peace with your inner self then release that person and let it go.

"Release and Let Go" Action Guideline

1. *Do not place new clothing on old garments.*
2. *Release and let go of ALL patterns that no longer serve you. Ask yourself, "Does this pattern serve me in my present situation or is it just a "pattern of nostalgia" that's justifying itself by its past works?*
3. *Change your physical activity patterns.*
4. *Meditate and pray. Connect with your true self to co-partner with the Omnipresent and Omnipotent Power to radiate new positive patterns and experiences in your life.*
5. *Know that ANYTHING that has been can be changed. Expect, very much expect, positive new changes to occur.*

CHAPTER 4
THE MATRIX VS. SELF-AWARENESS

This chapter will no doubt be the longest chapter in the book, because this is the *main* principle of all of the principles. The other six principles will be mastered as a result of *"The Matrix vs. Self-Awareness Principle."* Self-awareness is the key that unlocks the riches of life. We have all the answers we need to the questions of our lives right inside of us. All we have to do is learn how to access our own wisdom.

Most people today live in a world of fiction. Their minds are so cluttered with worry, doubt and fear that they are totally unaware that they are apart of a much greater universal reality. The masses in our society have evolved only to the point that they believe that their questions should be left for highly acclaimed theologians, philosophers and religious leaders. They believe that questions like "who am I and what is my purpose in this life?" is outside of their realm of intellect and have no place in the daily lives of the average individual. They have become inundated with the stories told to them by society, mis-education, erroneous parenting and media influence. Sadly enough, we believe these stories. These stories have caused us to limit ourselves in so many ways. We don't think we're good enough, we don't think we're educated enough, we believe we will become ill by a certain age because our parents or grandparents became ill at that same age and therefore we manifest the illness based on this false perception of our true being. STOP IT NOW!! Stop believing all of those stories. They're all fiction and they're limiting you from your *true potential.*

Most of us remember the movie *The Matrix* for its outstanding special effects, yet the story holds a distinct parallel to how we limit ourselves based on the fictional stories we've been told and how once we become *self-aware* and identify with our true spiritual selves we will have the power to defeat any situation. Keanu Reeves, who plays the main character, Neo, eventually mastered his own transformation by becoming self-aware and identifying with his true potential. Neo moved beyond the world he was living in, which was called the third-dimension consciousness, by practicing self-awareness and identifying with his true reality. His mission was to save the world from an invisible non-human enemy, an enemy that could not die. His comrades took him through a series of steps to help him realize who he really was, releasing him from the fictional stories that he'd been told so that he could perceive his true self and his destiny. Their goal was to show him the true powers of his mind, and teach him how to use them. Neo went from a desk job to another world of reality where he was trained to battle an unbeatable force, not just an unbeatable force, but an invisible unbeatable force and ultimately save the world. .

First his comrades showed him that the world he was living in came from the third dimension, which was called "The Matrix," a reality that existed only in his perception. In virtual reality settings, they took him beyond his third-dimension consciousness to show him that his failures came only from his worry, doubt and his uncertainty. They showed him that his power must first come from his belief in his true reality. He had to release his limitations and expand his mind. Neo first had to accept the concept that he was more than what he had always perceived himself to be and more than what he'd been told by society. He was taken to a woman called "The Oracle." She was what we would call a psychic or seer. The Oracle was to tell Neo if he was truly the savior of the human race. At her apartment, a little boy sat on the floor with a spoon. Neo watched the boy bend the spoon with his mind. Neo asked the boy how he did it, and the boy answered, "you must first realize the truth. The truth is; that there is no spoon". This has relevance later, and is the key to the movie and Neo's power.

When Neo went in to see the Oracle, he was not thinking anything positive about this experience and therefore he expected her to tell him he was *not* the chosen one. She looked him over, saw his uneasiness, and told him not to worry about the vase next to him. Just then he fidgeted and knocked the vase onto the floor, and it broke. He asked how she knew he was going to break it. She told him she didn't; she just suggested it (*the power of suggestion*). Then she told him that he is *not* the one who has been chosen to save the world. Of course, he readily accepted this and of course he got exactly what his *thoughts* dictated would happen. He held onto his belief in his limitations and he was not mentally ready to step beyond his comfort zone to become bigger than he thought himself to be. Later, when he battled the enemy, his skills had become slightly sharpened due to some lessons he'd learned, but the enemy was still more powerful than he. He continued to believe the fictional stories he'd been told, therefore his thoughts limited his ability to defeat the enemy. He failed because he allowed his thoughts to tell him that the enemy was more powerful than he. His comrades told him that he was faster, that he was better and that he was more powerful than they, and he responded, "you mean I can dodge bullets?", they replied, "I mean when you are ready, you won't have to". Neo first had to accept the concept that the power of the enemy lived in his thoughts, in his belief system but in reality in true *self-awareness*; the enemy does *not* exist. Later, he realized the reason the Oracle told him that he wasn't the chosen one was only because he wasn't ready at that time. He realized that when he changed his thoughts and beliefs in himself, when he realized he was better than the limitations he'd set upon himself, he was able to release them and became self-aware. He then saw himself at his full potential. This is when he took the step beyond the comfort zone of the Matrix, the only reality of what he had always known, to his higher potential. This is when he strengthened his mind and decided to battle the enemy and save his comrades.

After a blazing battle with guards on his way to rescue his comrade named Morpheus, Neo and another colleague, Trinity, clung to cable wires inside an elevator shaft. As he contemplated the rescue and the upcoming battle with the foes called the Agents, Neo whispered, "There is no spoon". Then he took off after the enemy. Here is where he realized what the boy who bent the spoon meant: that the enemy does not really exist, that it has no power except in what he grants it. He reached his highest potential when he completely released the limiting fictional stories of his true identity and became totally self-aware. It was at this moment that he knew he no longer had to fight back. He had attained the pinnacle of power. Neo was walking in *self-awareness*. His life was no longer governed by the fictional stories that had been told to him over the years. He finally believed in his full potential, and had the ability to see beyond the illusion (the worry, doubt and fear). He had *released it and let it go.*

If you haven't figured it out by now, I am a huge fan of *The Matrix*. This movie holds very true principles of how some of us are living our lives today. We're actually limiting our true potential by living in a Matrix of fictional stories that have been perpetuated over the years. By becoming self-aware, we can strip away the self-imposed limitations and began living a happy, successful life. No longer do you have to accept certain experiences in your life just because your mind has been trained by one source or another that it is so. If you're looking to make a career change and you've been mentally trained to believe that you only know how to do one type of work and if you're released from that type of work either due to layoff or termination, poverty will result. Come out of the Matrix and began to identify with your true identity and you will realize that there are no limitations to what you can accomplish. Don't allow your background or upbringing to dictate the type of person that you will marry or the type of person that you can meet or believe that a certain medicine is the only sure way to heal a physical condition.

Self-awareness is the first step to achieving your goals. It clears the track for transformation. As you grow in self-awareness, you will better understand why you feel what you feel and why you behave as you behave, and why and how you started on an emotional path that has caused you so much disappointment. You will begin to understand when and where those thoughts and behaviors first began to take shape in your life. You will know that it is not who you really are; understanding this gives you the opportunity and freedom to change those things you'd like

35

to change about yourself and create the life you really want. Without fully knowing who you are change become impossible.

Having clarity about who you really are empowers you to consciously and actively make those things you want and desire a reality, just like Neo. Once he identified with his true self and who he really was, he was able to overpower his enemy. If you do not practice self-awareness, you'll continue to get caught up in your own internal dramas and fictional stories, thereby allowing ungoverned thought processes to determine your feelings and actions and ultimately your experiences.

Take a minute and think about it. Not understanding why you do what you do, and why you feel what you feel, can be equated to going through your life with a stranger's mind. Not just one stranger, but many strangers. Although some of your thoughts were formally introduced by people you know (family, friends, etc.), many were formulated by total strangers, from people we read about in school, the media, our government and our religious leaders; most of these people we've never met. How can you make wise decisions and choices if you don't understand why you want what you want? It's a difficult and chaotic way to live, never knowing what this stranger is going to do next, especially if it was a thought that was formulated by a stranger over twenty years ago. The world is constantly evolving; life is constantly evolving, what worked twenty years ago may or may not apply to today, but if you are not walking in self-awareness and you do not know your true self, then your only frame of reference will be the mindset you adopted from that stranger over twenty years ago.

Generally, when we want good, solid information, we turn to the experts. We search the Internet, we go to libraries and we contact resources who are believed to be experts in the area of information that we are seeking. So who are you going to turn to for information about yourself? Who's the expert? You. You are the only one who knows about you. Does a friend, a therapist, a minister, your hero, your spouse, or your mother or father know more about you than you do? They can't. You live in your skin and mind 24 hours a day, 7 days a week, 52 weeks a year, day in and day out. No one's closer to you than you! There are people and information (such as this book) who can teach you the principles of self-awareness just as Morpheus taught Neo the principles, but you have to believe and accept that all of the Ennis to achieving a successful life are already within you.

Through becoming self-aware, being more cognizant of your personal relationship to the whole of life, you become more intellectually, and above all, more intuitively aware of how to guide your life toward more successful living. I suggest that you read this chapter twice; when read in depth it provides a combination of scientific, psychological and spiritual truths, which, if applied to your individual life, will indeed make life more successful by giving you a new consciousness of who and what you really are.

"The Matrix vs. Self-Awareness" Action Guideline

1. *STOP believing the fictional stories you've been told over the years. It's only a Matrix.*
2. *Believe and know that a higher power exists outside of the physical world in which you are living.*
3. *Believe and know that your true power lies in walking in Self-Awareness and identifying with your true oneness.*
4. *Believe and know that your challenges are not real and have no power over you. It's all made up based on the fictional stories of self-imposed limitations and by walking in self-awareness you ultimately have the power to defeat it.*
5. *Maintain calmness in the face of a challenging situation. By doing so you will be able to think rationally and realize that you have the ultimate control over the situation.*
6. *Take care of anything you have been putting off due to fear and self-doubt that are based on the beliefs of the fictional stories you've been told.*
7. *When in the presence of others; think, act and speak as a person who is walking in self-awareness and who is in control of his or her life. At first it may seem like a performance, but soon this vibration will become a natural part of you which will set in motion the right conditions through which you realize that you have control over your life.*
8. *Watch The Matrix !!*
9. *Remember daily who you are. Before you arise each morning and before you go to sleep each night remember:* You are a child of the Divine, with a right to be free of self-imposed limitations, with a right to walk in true self-awareness, with a right to know for yourself who you really are. You are a Divine heir to the riches in a Universal Kingdom. The essence of your true identity is one with the Divine and one with Omnipotence. Your true identity is your reality and not the fictional stories you've read or the stories you've been told.

Read this daily for seven days, then periodically as needed.

CHAPTER 5

TRANSFORMATION

As a child, I was fascinated with *The Wizard of Oz*. Oddly enough, I never watched much television as a child, yet every year, I knew the exact date and time of the airing of the 1939 MGM movie *The Wizard of Oz*. I was always an avid reader and the book fair was my favorite school event. It was at my fourth-grade book fair that I discovered the Oz books, and I was excited to learn that the movie wasn't the whole story. In fact, it wasn't even the "true" story, because the movie concluded that everything had been a dream; that there was no wizard, no Emerald City, no Land of Oz, when in actuality for L. Frank Baum, the creator of Oz, the Land of Oz was very real.

Even as a ten-year old I was very curious to learn more about L. Frank Baum and his magical writings. Luckily for my parents, we didn't have the internet back then; because I would've certainly been a cyber addict, however, we did have the *Encyclopedia Britannica*, and reading encyclopedias was my favorite pastime. I'd go through one entire volume in a week. The encyclopedia salesman loved coming to our home because my mother would have to purchase not only the upgraded editions but also the accompanying reference books. I did as much research as I could on L. Frank Baum and the Emerald City, but back then the information was very limited, so my psyche on that subject was never quite satisfied. The story always remained a distant memory of a heavenly place; even after I grew up.

While a very good friend was getting his master's degree in psychology, he mentioned that one of his classmates presented a very interesting psychological theory on Dorothy and *The Wizard of Oz*. We discussed it briefly and my interest was immediately rekindled as if it were only yesterday that I'd first seen the movie. I immediately began to replay the entire story in mind.

Now, many years later; after much study as a spiritual teacher, I fully understand why the movie, the books and encyclopedia readings had captivated me. I realized that *The Wizard of Oz* was more than an imaginative adventure. The journey down the yellow brick road is a quest, a journey of self-discovery, as each character discovers that the true source of what they seek is within. The wizard can't help them; he can only point to the truth that they must find within themselves.

Transformation does not come from fixing yourself up. It arises from the extraordinary discovery that you are already whole from the realization of your true self. It's a complete change in your experience of how you relate to yourself and subsequently the world around you.

Ask yourself if you really have a desire to change. Do you really believe it's necessary for you to change, or do you think that nothing is wrong with you and that everyone else around you should change? If you decide it is necessary, do you believe you're determined enough to stick it out until the total change takes place? These questions are solely intended to put you in a corner, to back you up to where you have to choose between yes or no. For some people, to be backed into a corner is the only way they will come to a point in their life where they will move forward toward transformation, hence the "law of self preservation"; which states, when a person is backed into a corner he has no choice, but make a decision to protect himself. The purpose of these questions has been to help you go deep inside and corner yourself, and to stop avoiding the changes that you know you should have made a long time ago.

The main reason that people fail within the transformation process is because they believe there's always a "Plan B" or an alternative course to follow, so they prefer to take the road most traveled and avoid making those changes that they know are necessary. Generally, it is not until a person's circumstances or emotions dictate to them, "you can't do this any more, you have to make a change," that the person will become serious about making the necessary changes for true transformation.

One of the first things we must attain while on the road to Oz is to have a love and knowledge of the truth. We are all familiar with the biblical expression, "Know the truth and the truth shall make you free." Seeking the truth begins with being curious about what is going on in ourselves and around us, not settling for the programmed answers that we're fed by both ourselves and our society. If we take the time to really observe our behaviors and responses, we will see that many of the explanations that we give ourselves for our behavior and for the actions of others are a form of denial and avoidance of truth.

By learning to accept what is real in the present moment, makes us more willing to acknowledge whatever behaviors or thoughts we project, because we know that is not the whole of who we are. It is a combination of our Matrix experience combined with our true self. While our programmed responses can derail our quest for the truth, taking ownership of their presence in most instances will bring us closer to the truth. When you are willing to see the whole truth, whether it is the truth as seen in your Matrix experience or the authentic truth of your true self, you still have the responsibility to take ownership that it is so for that moment. Remember in Principle 4, there were two truths that existed within Neo simultaneously; he knew that the reason the Oracle didn't see him as the chosen one was because he was not ready to accept the responsibility, and that his thoughts were still governed by worry, doubt and fear. That was the present moment of truth of his Matrix experience and he had to accept it in order to move forward into his new found truth and ultimate transformation.

A central truth advocated in the New Testament is known as the Gospel of the Kingdom of Heaven. It states that heaven is not a place that you go after you die, but rather the living presence of the Spirit at the center of your being. This truth is the reality of who you truly are. Accepting this truth is the ultimate source of power. By accepting this and practicing the daily connection with the indwelling spirit you will see that you do not have to look outside yourself for transformation, because just like Dorothy in the land of Oz, what you need is already within you.

Now, you can choose (remember we make choices) to accept this truth or not. Perhaps you've never experienced this type of connection in your prayer, meditation or moments of quiet reflections. Nevertheless, truth still makes itself known in many other ways, whether it is the words of a beautiful song or a phone call from a friend that you've been thinking of. Okay, so you say, "I know this truth, so now what?" I wish I could tell you that's all it takes, but it's not; you also have to live this truth. You have to walk and talk in the knowingness that there's a part of you that is connected to a spiritual realm that transcends anything in your present Matrix experience. Once you're walking in this oneness; your transformation has arrived and you will be begin to effortlessly and harmoniously create your own environment.

Living each day by the ultimate truth taught in Principle 5 can and will allow you to create positive experiences beyond anything you've ever dreamed or imagined possible.

"Transformation" Action Guideline

1. *Know that the true source of what you're seeking can be found within.*

2. *Know that you do not have to "fix yourself." You are already whole. You only have to connect with your true self to remember who you really are, a perfect person created in the loving image of all that is perfect.*

3. *Enforce the "law of self-preservation." Back yourself into a corner and force yourself to make a decision to change.*

4. *Be completely willing to change to follow through in the knowledge that if a change is going to be made in one's life it must really begin within oneself.*

5. *Recognize that transforming oneself inwardly may be one of the most challenging undertakings in your adult life.*

6. *Know and realize that through this transformation you <u>will</u> suffer the inevitable loss of some friends or people who were once close to you. It's all part of the process.*

7. *As you begin your change process, do not look down on others who are less enlightened. Remember you were once there also.*

8. *You must accept that on some level there is a spiritual power that is higher than yourself.*

9. *Realize that while spiritual leaders and psychotherapists are able guides, understand that they are only guides. The real decision to change must take place within oneself.*

10. *Rent* The Wizard of Oz. *Watch it twice.*

11. *"Know the truth and the truth shall make you free."*

CHAPTER 6

THE SOURCE

A new spiritual awakening is occurring in human culture, an awakening brought on by individuals who experience their lives as a spiritual unfolding. Unfortunately, on the other hand, there is a greater mass of individuals who have not yet come to this realization and believe that life is a struggle, because they believe that they are aligned against the powers that be. This is a totally fictitious thought that runs rampant in our society. Not only is life not intended to be a struggle, but once you learn to connect to the source; you will have a co-creator to assist you in creating the life you've always wanted. Most people, because they are not aware of this truth, unnecessarily take the full responsibility to undertake life's challenges. It is my intent to demonstrate to you in this chapter how to connect to the source, the presence, and the power in your *own* life so that you too can identify with this statement and discover the success associated with these 7 Principles of the ages.

Your body and mind is the location for the power of divine Spiritual Intelligence to reside. Your true spiritual self, which was created in the exact same image of the Spiritual Intelligence I'm speaking of. It's this simple: by getting and staying in touch with your true spiritual being, which is, the exact same as, staying connected to the source. God as most would say, Spiritual Intelligence called by many as well is spirit and if we are to have the full knowledge of the source we must know and spend quality time with the source in spirit and in truth. In order for the reality of the oneness with God to become greater than your present expectations, you must synthesize your mind with the mind of God that is within you. Understand and realize that there is only one source in this universe from which all other energies and human thought forms come regardless to what name you choose to call it; it's only one source. This one source has existed throughout eternity and occupies infinity at the physical level as well as other dimensional levels. It is omniscient, omnipotent, omnipresent, and has no beginning and no end. The Source is at the center of the heart and mind of all things that exist, whether animate or inanimate. It is Spirit—not "a spirit" but Spirit. Remember Jesus The Christ said, "God is Spirit and those who worship Him must worship Him in spirit and in truth." To say that God is "a spirit" would imply that there are many spirits; Jesus did not imply this. Many of us have been taught to believe that God is this "person" with a long, white beard, who sits on a throne in some distant sky and dictates what we should and should not do. In actuality, God is not *out there* and the Kingdom of Heaven is not *out there.* It is right here in you. God is spirit that is within you. The Kingdom of Heaven is in you; therefore your objective in your transformation is to awaken and connect with the source that's already in you. God is not a noun, not a person having love, life, power, intelligence, wisdom; God is love, God is life, God is power, intelligence and wisdom. God is the invisible behind all that is manifest. Simply stated, God *is.*

We have come forth out of God. We are a threefold being, made up of a spirit, soul or mind, and a body. Spirit, the true self that I've been speaking about throughout this book, has never changed. It is the same today, yesterday and forever. However, we in our physical body and mind have forgotten who we really are at the core of our being, which is, our true spiritual selves. This is the "I" of us, the Father within us. At the true core of our spiritual being every person can say, "My Father and I are one," and speak the absolute truth. The soul or the mind which the Apostle Paul called the mortal mind of the flesh is where our conscious thinking resides; finally, the body is the external part of man's being, in his descent from God into the material universe.

So far what I've explained is called *Transcendent Awareness.* By regularly practicing transcendent awareness you can connect to the true source and have full insight and access to your life's direction. You can also create your experiences as you would wish them to occur. You will then realize that you have an unlimited supply of power to make all of your endeavors a success. Notice that I said you will realize that you have the power within you, not that you will find the power or the power will come, because the power of God's Spirit has always existed within you. However, the existence of power is of no value unless we use it, so the first step is to become conscious that it exists.

The further intention of this principle is to provide you with sensitivity techniques whereby you will learn how to effortlessly turn your mind over to the source within while going about your daily lives. The goal is for you to be able to connect to the source at any given time. This may sound a little frightening at first. You may think this means you're being asked to give up who you really are, when in actuality you will be only spending less time with the fictitious person that has been manufactured through years of erroneous teachings.

The self that I'm asking you to spend less time with is the self that has caused you so many challenges. It's the self that has created all of the unpleasant circumstances in your life. Once you get used to spending time away from that person, trust me, you won't miss him or her. The true self—God Self—that you will be spending more time with is the one who has brought you out of those challenging circumstances in your darkest hour. It's the one who made a way for you when you didn't see your way. The God-Self is the one who has come forward in those split moments when you felt that you'd been truly blessed and you know that based on your actions, thoughts and behaviors, you do not rightfully deserve it. So don't worry, you will not lose all sense of identity once you begin the regular practice of connecting with the source.

Let me explain how it is that you can learn to connect with the Source, your true self who is all spirit, and at the same time still maintain your current personal identity, the one that you've grown accustomed to. As I mentioned earlier, even in our darkest hour there were times when you still were able to see the light at the end of the tunnel. There were times when a thought or grand idea entered your mind that you never dreamed of; this idea ended up being the one that changed your life. Perhaps it was purchasing this book. Well, that's because God has never left you; your God-Self is always there observing you every step of the way. Remember I said that man is a three-part being, spirit, mind or soul, and body. Because it's three parts in one, one or another can always observe the characteristics of the others. The same applies even at the height of your connection with the source; your current personality, the one that has caused you all of the troubles, is still close enough to observe. The purpose of this ability is so that it can learn to transform its character and become more and more conscious in your daily activities of your true purpose in life. The more time you stay connected to the source, the more your current personality will observe, and at some point it will become natural for you to walk in abundance, in total harmony and in love. Your spirit will find fulfillment through this practice, which is ultimately God's fulfillment, which is ultimately the fulfillment of your true self.

Jesus was able to discern and transform a spiritual idea back to its physical symbol. He knew and realized the great truth that it is not really our business (personal, self, ego), but it is the purpose of the one God, the True Spirit that is the true business of life and that we are only an embodiment positioned to carry out that purpose. Through this practice of connecting with the Source, you will come to experience what Jesus taught and what Buddha and many other enlightened spiritual leaders taught throughout the ages; that the personal and the universal God-Self can function harmoniously together throughout one's life. Jesus simply stated, "My Father and I are ONE." Please note that once you began to regularly practice connecting to the Source it will not mean that suddenly you will be speaking in "holier than thou" terms. It's more of a state of mind, a state of peace, a sense of knowing that nothing will catch you off guard any more. You will have discernment of situations. You will be able to maintain your composure, which will become visible in your expression, and in your tone, which will allow you to communicate wisdom to another person in a way they will understand. Also, and this one is very important, for some reason people seem to think that once one becomes spiritually enlightened, awakened or connected to the

Source that they will no longer raise their voice and appear to get angry. In extreme instances, you may raise your voice or appear indignant in order to make a point on a level that another person's evolvement may understand. If your God-Self is truly at the helm during this time, you will experience no part of what outwardly appears to be an indignant vibration; internally you will remain in a state of peace. I know that this sounds too good to be true, but trust me, immediately after you complete the book you will have an opportunity to demonstrate to yourself the power of being connected.

The 7 Principles to this power resides in daily meditation and prayer. No one can grow in spiritual knowledge, true wisdom, or fully tap into and experience the manifestations of the world that they desire to create without it. We must practice the presence of God and spend time with the true self, just as an athlete competing for a major competition would practice to win. I read that Tiger Woods practices every morning for hours in order to constantly improve his game. Tiger is also a strong believer in meditation and visualization; he uses visualization almost constantly while on the golf course. Often, other golfers have accused Tiger of not being social while playing because most other golfers are chatting while on the course. What they don't know is that he's not being rude or antisocial; he's meditating and visualizing his next shot. These practices along with his dedicated work ethic are the reasons that he's dominated this sport from the day he turned professional. Tiger Woods, a champion golfer, would never dream of attempting to win the Masters without fervent dedication, focus and practice. The same applies in your winning at the game of life; in order to master life's challenge and totally control the green in your life, you will need to spend time in meditation and prayer. You may think you're so busy doing and helping others that you've accomplished your God-given duties; however, there's more to it than that. Those are only works; you need to spend time with your spiritual being, your true self, even if it means putting aside some of the tasks for others.

Through daily prayer and meditation; I now welcome you to the greatest way of living your life. Fervent practice of prayer and meditation will cause many of your dreams to become realities. The power you will learn through meditation is the same power that Jesus Christ as well as many other spiritual sages have taught and practiced. How is this so, you ask? Because meditation will ultimately connect you with God, and Spiritual Knowledge will give you the power to transcend the physical world in many ways, from healing others to spiritual discernment. If this is your first time practicing meditation, consider yourself blessed as a whole new world and concept, your potential, is about to open up to you. You will not only discover that the power to have the life you've always wanted is within you, but even more importantly you will learn how to use it and apply it to every area of your life that you would like to see improved. No matter how much you read and how much you study, it means nothing if you can't apply the knowledge toward improving your own life, then the lives of others around you.

Meditation is practiced by taking time each day, fifteen minutes to an hour, and going into your own mind. Here's the catch: You're not going into your mind to think, but to release your everyday thoughts so that your deeper consciousness (spirit man) will come forth and become very apparent to you. You will know and operate from the mind of the spirit instead of from the mind of your current personality. The practice is done with your eyes closed. Although your physical eyes will be closed, there's another eye that we all have; it's called the third eye or the eye of the soul. As you begin to practice, you will discover this second sight. Your mind will begin to see into itself. This is what Jesus referred to when He said, "If thine eye be single, the body shall be filled with Light". Many enlightened spiritual leaders throughout history have been aware of this second sight; they have used it to discover the presence and ultimate reality of God.

There are many methods of meditation and to connecting to source. I will show you a simple format, which will allow you to easily begin this practice.

1. Select a time of day and a place in your home where you will have uninterrupted peace and quiet.

2. Dress very comfortably: loose-fitting clothing, preferably linen or cotton, no belts. I also recommend light solid colors. I suggest no shoes if appropriate. Your aim is to be as free-spirited as possible, even prior to beginning your meditation.

3. Sit in an upright position with your back straight. You can sit on the floor against a sofa or wall as long as you have something to support your back, or you can sit in a chair at a table or a desk. I prefer sitting on the floor with a table in front of me.

4. Place a single white candle on the table in front of you (optional).

5. Take about 10 minutes and intently look at the flame of the burning candle. This time should be estimated; it's not necessary to look at your watch. The candle should be about 12 inches from your head. The purpose of this is to initiate focus and concentration so you can steady your mind, focus it and shut out all of the day's activities. Once you done this several times you may no longer need the candle as a focus point.

6. After approximately 10 minutes you may close your eyes.

7. If you have been looking at the candle intently for about 10 minutes you should now continue to see the image of the candle flame in your soul's eye. This is appearing in the interior region of your forehead. This will be the first spiritually enlightened experienced with your spirit being. You will actually be able to see the same flame as if your eyes are open. Continue to remain focused on this flame.

8. This image will begin to fade out after a few minutes, and may also fade in and out. What's important to note is that at this time you are actually using this image as an inner point of concentration. Remember your physical eyes are now closed, but you're still able to see the last thing you were focused on prior to closing them. This means you have shifted from an outer concentration point to an inner concentration point which will make you more aware of the spirit at the core of your true self.

9.   After the image of the candle has totally faded from your soul's eye, continue to sit still and look further into your inner consciousness; at this point all of the thoughts and activities of the day should have faded.

During this time you may experience cloud-like formations of color, pictures of various things in flat or dimensional appearances, and an inner light. The pictures that one sees are coming from many different places. Now that you are no longer attuned to the thoughts and activities of day-to-day life, your conscious is open to many different planes. You will see images from the subconscious mind, which is basically your mind's memory of everything you've ever experienced. Other images you may see are religious symbols of all kinds, crosses, a Star of David, etc. Do not be startled if you see a Jesus-like image in your mind, or even what you may perceive as Jesus. This means you have gone beyond the ordinary awareness of the human mind. You may see an inner light which is often referred to as astral light; astral light is somewhat limited in its perception, because you still have a sense of person self-hood. The ultimate experience is when you see the inner light that we all should strive for in meditation; in this experience, all sense of self-hood and your current personality and all of its drama vanishes and is replaced with a sense of oneness with God. In this experience there is no sense of a physical body; there is just a oneness with what you will be able to fully comprehend once you experience this inner light.

Meditate for about 10 minutes. After you have meditated for a few days, the amount of time can be increased to 30 minutes if you desire. This will be an experience like never before. I guarantee you that once you begin, you will notice *immediate* changes. You will see results of your meditation the very next day and if you meditate in the mornings before starting your day, you will see results the exact same day. Meditation and prayer is one of the quickest ways to connecting with and maintaining contact with God, You are not to be as concerned with the experiences of your meditations, apart from being a source of knowledge, spiritual insight and creativity, as evidence that a Higher Intelligence, Spiritual Mind that resides within you can be contacted and that its power and intelligence can be manifested and demonstrated in our daily life. As you begin to spend more time in meditation and prayer your true Spiritual Self and the Omnipresent, Omnipotent Power takes hold of your life, and many things will quickly begin to take place. You should immediately begin to notice that relationships with family, friends and co-workers will begin to improve, people will become more drawn to you, you will become more optimistic about life and your current circumstances, intuition will begin to guide your actions and you will feel more in control of your conditions, you will have a sense of knowing that nothing is as it appears to your physical eyes, and you will become more creative, more motivated and increasingly more intuitively aware of the motivations of others. In short, through the practice of daily meditation you will know without a doubt that God, who has all power and all knowledge, and at last you are in control of your life.

"The Source" Action Guideline

1. Know that you are not alone in your endeavors.
2. Know that your mind and body are a place for the Spirit of God. You were created in the image of a Omnipotent, Omnipresent, All Knowing God..
3. Know that your true spiritual self was created in the image of God so at a deeper level you are connected to the Source.
4. Know that God is Spirit and in order to know, experience the knowledge and magnificence, and manifest that power, you must connect in spirit and in truth.
5. Know that meditation and prayer are the Ennis to staying connected to Spirit.
6. Know that just as a championship golfer needs to practice and spend time with his or her game to win, so must you spend uninterrupted time with Spirit to win in the game of life.
7. Know that meditation will change your life forever and give you instant power and access to spiritual knowledge.
8. Know that through meditation you will receive a "second sight," an ability to see beyond your human experience.
9. Begin by spending 10 minutes per day in deep meditation.
10. Identify a quiet place in your home where you will be uninterrupted for an extended period of time.
11. Light a white candle and place it on a table at least 12 inches in front of you.
12. Concentrate on the flame for 10 minutes.
13. After 10 minutes, close your physical eyes and begin to see with your soul's eyes.
14. Sit still and quietly as you begin to experience different images and sights.
15. After 10 minutes, take a deep breath. Inhale, exhale.
16. Know that you are now becoming a truly complete person, one who is inwardly aware and outwardly successful, through the power that you access by connecting with the Source.

Chapter 7
Living The Life You Want

This is my favorite chapter. It's time to begin living the life you've always wanted; you now possess the 7 Principles of the ages. You now share the same knowledge as many enlightened spiritual leaders throughout history. The purpose of this chapter is to assist you in achieving your desires. Notice this is the first time I've used the phrase achieving your "desires." It was important that you first understand the importance of right thoughts and right actions prior to achieving your heart's desires. Remember you've been creating circumstances in your life all along; you just have not been conscious of it, so you've been creating experiences that you did not want. Now that you've learned to control your thoughts and guide your spiritual life and that the world we live in is not real in the sense of who we really are, but just a matrix of what the human experience has created for us, you've released the self-imposed limitations. Now you can directly connect to the Source to receive the spiritual knowledge to consciously and knowingly begin living the life you've always wanted.

Whatever your goals, needs or desires in life at this moment, you can have them. This chapter will be strictly about making choices and taking actions. Do not look at where you are currently, but look at where you want to be. If it is your desire to be a gourmet chef, but you are currently a homemaker or a waiter in a restaurant, view yourself only as a gourmet chef. Acquaint yourself with other gourmet chefs and prepare only gourmet meals in your home. Regardless of your budget, you can still prepare food in ways that will make it look as though it was prepared by a gourmet chef. Basically, what I'm saying is that you must be able to "see it" to "believe it," and once you believe it and meditate on it by following the 7 principles; it will manifest into reality. Surround yourself with people who support you in your dream; in fact, share your dream only with people who you know share your same vision for your life. Be careful to make sure that it is your dream that you are desiring and not someone else's. For example, let's say your parents always wanted you to become a teacher, and that's what you've become. You've always wanted to be an artist, but instead of visualizing yourself as an artist and looking into taking art classes, you are further pursuing a higher degree in teaching. In this case, it's not really your dream you're living, but that of your parents. Let's say your spouse and children feel that you're the world's greatest mom and wife. All of your friends and family compliment you on what a lovely home you keep and how well-mannered your kids are; the neighborhood moms look to you as Mother of the Year. You're flattered and continue to meet their expectations year after year. However, you've been yearning to return to college and get the degree you never finished. Again, you're not creating your dreams and desires; you're actually creating the dreams of your spouse, children, family and friends. Do not allow guilt or a sense of obligation to keep you from creating your own dreams.

Now let's talk about actions. You must put into action those things that you are desiring. No matter how small the effort, it's the effort that counts. Remember all things that are manifested and materialized were once only a thought. The more energy you put into them in action and in deed, the more quickly they will materialize. So if you desire to be a gourmet chef, begin by taking a cooking class. It doesn't have to be anything elaborate; you can take a class at a local community college. What's important is that you've begun the process of creating your desires. You're initiating the action and putting the energy in motion to manifest into something greater. Basically what you will need to do in order to create the life you want is to apply all seven principles that you've learned in this book. You are to use all of your energy to bring about those things which you want. By re-focusing on each principle you are setting the perfect condition to begin manifesting your desires. By following each of the action guidelines you are setting up an inner environment for God's Omnipotent Power to work in and through you.

You will notice that what we have called miracles throughout the ages will begin to occur in your life. This is a true sign that your life is aligned with the Universal Principles of the highest. In this principle you will also experience the process of evolution. As you evolve; your spiritual intuition will also evolve; you will be able to manifest your thoughts more quickly, depending on the level of your evolvement. It is also important with Principle 7 to release and let go of any expectations. Know that you can't have any predefined notions or thoughts of how the dreams will be manifested; you have to just let it happen. More than likely it will not materialize through the avenue that you believe it will.

Your mental atmosphere is key when it comes to creating your desires. It is important in Principle 7 that you incorporate your daily mental thought patterns with the spiritual thoughts that you receive during meditation. You will be required in this principle to incorporate affirmations in your meditation practice. Affirmations are aimed at the subconscious, the memory bank of the mind, the area that holds all of the self-imposed limitations, erroneous programming and negative experiences that have occurred over the years. While operating in our human state, utilizing your day-to-day personality, the subconscious mind governs over 90% of your conscious decision-making. Affirmations are a form of auto-suggestion in which a statement of a desirable intention or condition of the mind is deliberately meditated on or repeated in order to implant the newly desired result. An affirmation is a very powerful means of reprogramming the unconscious mind. The reason this is important in this stage is because the condition or state of one's conscious mental attitude must be open and clear of negative static; it must be receptive to receive the creativity that's trying to enter in from your true spirit self and the Omnipotent Power which has been opened though the process of meditation and prayer. While the practice of meditation will allow you to connect to the Source and receive spiritual guidance and insight, the act of affirmations will equip you with the tools to remain positive, receptive and intuitively open while going about your day-to-day business.

Day by day you will begin to realize that the personal mind has a companion in the Higher God-Mind or Spirit. By staying attuned with this higher level of consciousness through your meditation and affirmations, the realization comes to you that you are not alone, that you are being directed and guided and that it is easier than you think to begin to create the life you want. It is this inner knowing and relationship with a higher power that makes us take action in our lives. Your thoughts and desires will only be as valuable as the actions you put behind them. There's a biblical scripture that says, "Faith without works is dead." This scripture disturbed the Father of the Protestant Church, Martin Luther, so much that he considered throwing out the book of James in its entirety. The Protestant Church and many others are thankful that he didn't. See, while Martin Luther was still a young Roman Catholic priest, he taught the doctrine of justification by faith and this scripture in James was totally contrary to his teaching, at least at first glance. After careful study, Martin Luther realized that the scripture was correct, and was saying that you can have all the faith in the world, you can be equipped with right thoughts and you could be well on your way to creating the life you want, but if you don't put action behind it, it doesn't mean anything, or in this case it will not manifest. The action brought forth from the inspirational silence of meditation and from your affirmations will be the key to creating your life's desires.

Here are 7 Simple Affirmations that you can use to assist you in the process of creating your desires. As you become more comfortable with these affirmations you will notice how easy it is to make your own as the situation arises.

Before You Begin
- Decide what area of your life you want to work on and then decide what you want. There are several important points to know about affirmations:
- Use the present or past tense. Do not use the future tense. You want your mind to know it has already happened.

- Be POSITIVE. Use the most positive terms you can. Never use negatives in affirmations.
- Write them. As you are learning to do affirmations, write them down so you will remember exactly what you want to say. Keep them short and very specific. Personalize them with your name.
- Believe. Always believe that what you are saying is happening. The more you believe, the stronger the affirmation.
- Repetition. Being repetitive and persistent helps to set them in your head and in your unconscious being.
- Time. Always have a specific time daily set aside for your meditations, affirmations and visualizations. This will help set a pattern for you so you will do them daily.

Affirmations for Spiritual Awareness
- I am always connected to Divine love.
- My life has great purpose and meaning.
- I am safe and always feel protected.
- I am a loving and forgiving person.
- I choose to let my light shine forth from my being.
- I choose to let the doorway of my higher spiritual self fully open so that Divine knowledge may flow.
- I am responsible for my own spiritual growth.

Affirmations for Relationships
- I am happy and I only attract people into my life that share my vision for life.
- I am no longer looking for the right person. I am becoming the right person..
- I am a whole person, capable of an open, loving relationship. I love and care for my body and my body loves and cares for me.
- As I learn to please myself, I can have more natural and honest relationships.

Affirmations for Health

- I am happy, I am healthy, and the presence of my higher spiritual consciousness flows through me.
- My body is healthy and functioning the way that God intended.
- I do not fear being healthy because I know that I control my own body through my relationship and connection to source.
- I love and care for my body and my body loves and cares for me.
- I am surrounded by love at all times. Love flows through me.

Affirmations for Wealth

- Wealth is pouring into my life at this very moment.
- I am respected for my abilities and will always work to my full capacity.
- I'm one with the Spiritual Truth, where all abundance lives.
- I'm successful in whatever I do.
- I always spend my finances wisely.

Affirmations for Peace of Mind

- Peace is all around me.
- Love is all round me.
- I have provided a harmonious place for myself and for those whom I love.
- My thoughts are under control.
- I am calm and relaxed in every situation.

"Create What You Want" Action Guideline

1. First make a choice, then take action.
2. Do not look at where you are currently, look at where you want to be.
3. See it in your mind first, so you can believe it.
4. Surround yourself with people who are positive and share your desires.
5. Only speak your desires to people who you are sure will support you.
6. Be sure that you are creating your dream and not someone else's.
7. TAKE ACTION.
8. Ensure that your mental atmosphere is prime for creating your desires.
9. Practice daily meditations and affirmations.
10. Remember that you are what you think.

CONCLUSION

Sharing these principles with you has been an extraordinary experience and one of the greatest accomplishments of my life. When I started writing this book in 2004, my intent was to have it completed in three months. What I did not know at that time was that my own personal spiritual unfoldment would play a role in the completion of the book. There were days, weeks, months when I couldn't write a word on a page until I received clarity and complete understanding of the principle on which I was writing. That clarity and understanding always came through meditation and prayer.

I have made a commitment to continue to share these principles with all who come across my path and I would ask that you do the same.

ABOUT THE AUTHOR

Pamela Ennis, Ph.D., LPC, Certified Life Coach

Pamela is an Author, Teacher, Life Coach and Motivational Speaker who speaks from a combination of her own leadership experience and professional training. She's spent over 12 years as a Corporate Consultant and has held numerous Executive Leadership positions with some of the industries most respected companies. With her unique style of delivery, solid content and practical application, Pamela continues to motivate and inspire audiences with her wisdom, charismatic style, humorous insights and contagious positive energy.

Pamela currently resides in Houston, Texas, with her three children, Serigne, Solomon and Sarah.

APPENDIX

Affirmations – a positive statement affirming or asserting something to help manifest it in the physical world.

Astral Light – the nonphysical light perceived as vibrations surrounding beings or objects.

Astrophysicists – scientists who study the physics of the universe, including the physical properties of celestial objects such as stars, galaxies, and the interstellar medium, as well as their interactions.

Awakened – a human perception and cognitive reaction to a condition or event. To be awakened does not necessarily imply understanding—just an ability to be conscious of, feel or perceive.

Awareness – 1. Spiritual or higher consciousness; 2. not using the mind to look for reality.

Buddha – "awakened one". 1. Siddartha Gautama, chief personage of historic Buddhism, also known as Sakyamuni or sage of the Sakya tribe, c. 623-543; 2. principle of enlightenment; 3. an enlightened being, in any realm.

Eastern – ancient Asian culture, typically also including those countries whose ethnic identity and their dominant culture derive from ancient Asian culture.

Energy – metaphysically may be used synonymously with Life or Spirit, as in "Divine Energy". Often used with reference to inherent power.

God – 1. *(Judeo-Christianity)* creator and sustainer of the universe; 2. *(Theosophy)* transcendent and immanent being who guides and controls the course of planetary evolution; 3. sum total of all that is; 4. *(Islam)* Lord of the universe who cannot be represented by any form; 5. *(Hinduism)* The One who plays the game of life by becoming the Many, losing itself in the creation and finding its way back to unity; supreme being, personal friend, teacher, and lover who knows the heart of all beings; 6. *(mysticism)* indwelling spirit within all beings; one's highest self realized through contemplation or service; eternal, infinite, all-wise, all-knowing, all-loving, ever-free radiant presence; 7. *(humanism)* impersonal spirit of selfless love.

God-Self – inner voice, higher self.

Karma – the sum and the consequences of a person at any time during any of the life spans (incarnations on earth). Assumes reincarnation to be fact. The recorded accounting for all good, evil and indifference accompanies the entity and is a determiner of the soul's destiny in subsequent reincarnations. Karma is constantly created; natural law of Cause and Effect.

Manifestation – a term often used in New Thought and New Age circles to refer to the belief that one can by force of will, desire, and focused energy make something come true on the physical.

Meditation – a state in which to place the body and mind, the physiological and psychological selves, in preparation for the occurrence of relaxation and psi. The person is in a relaxed physical and mental state, where strain is replaced by passivity.

Omnipotent – (literally "all power") having power with no limits or which is inexhaustible; in other words, unlimited power. Monotheistic religions generally attribute omnipotence only to God.

Omnipresent – the ability to be present in every place at any and/or every time; unbounded or universal presence. It is related to the concept of ubiquity, the ability to be everywhere at a certain point in time.

Prayer – the deliberate attempt to center ourselves in conversations with God or deity of choice; the concentration of heart and mind that brings that communion.

Psychic – 1. realm of the paranormal, occult, or astral; 2. a person who is sensitive or responsive to etheric, spirit, or other nonphysical powers or manifestation.

Religion – a system of social coherence based on a common group of beliefs or attitudes concerning an object, person, unseen being, or system of thought considered to be supernatural, sacred, divine or highest truth, and the moral codes, practices, values, institutions, and rituals associated with such belief or system of thought.

Spiritual – having to do with the evolving soul, distinguished from "religious" dogmas and teachings by following the promptings and personal teachings of the spirit within self.

Third Eye – a metaphysical and esoteric concept referring in part to the ajna (brow) chakra in certain eastern and western spiritual traditions. In New Age spirituality, the third eye may alternately symbolize a state of enlightenment or the evocation of mental images having deeply personal spiritual or psychological significance. The third eye is often associated with visions, clairvoyance, precognition, and out-of-body experiences; people who have developed the capacity to use their third eyes are sometimes known as *seers*. Organ of intuition, located between the eyebrows; sixth chakra. The etheric correspondence of the pineal gland which sees, creates, communicates, heals, destroys obstacles, unveils mysteries, and controls and directs energies.

Transformation – an extreme psychological or character change usually as the result of an event, occurrence or mental enlightenment.

Universal – a law, concept or rule that applies unquestionably to any situation or circumstance.

Visualization – the process of forming positive thoughts or images, as a means of creating wellness.

Wisdom – 1. intuitive knowledge of the mind of love and clarity that lies beneath one's ego-driven anxieties and aggressions; 2. an advanced level of comprehension. Steps taught in spiritual understanding are information (data and concepts), knowledge (use of), and wisdom (the ability to synthesize, to see spiritual relationships). The dedicated observation and practice of knowledge results in wisdom.

INDEX